The Great Dinosaur Race

sundance

Meet Harry.

(He's so big we can't quite
fit him in.)

Meet Dodo.

(She fits in easily.)

Contents

CHAPTER 1

Harry the Bully

Harry was the biggest dinosaur of them all. When he walked, the earth shook and leaves fell from the trees.

"Move over! Here comes Harry," he always yelled.

And if other dinosaurs didn't jump out of the way, he walked on their tails.

Harry never said, "Excuse me."
It never entered his mind that he
should. And when he wanted
something, he never said,
"Please," or "Thank you."

He just took what he wanted.
Nobody argued, of course.
How could they, when Harry
could flatten them with one
flick of his tail?

No, they just limped away,
pretending that they didn't
mind being pushed around.

Dodo was one of the smallest dinosaurs. She was very quiet and always said things like, "I do hope you don't mind," or "How very kind of you."

Dodo didn't like Harry. She didn't like the way he acted toward the other dinosaurs, and she hated the way he shouted all the time. She didn't argue back with him though, because she didn't like being walked on either.

But Dodo thought about it a lot. "It isn't fair," she told herself. "Being the biggest shouldn't mean that you get your own way all the time. And it doesn't mean that you are the best at everything either."

However, Harry seemed to think that it did. "I'm the best at simply EVERYTHING!" he always shouted. "Nobody is as good as I am."

And of course they wouldn't disagree because they didn't want their poor, sore tails stomped on.

CHAPTER 2
Dodo's Idea

One day, while Dodo was sitting watching Harry push everyone around, she suddenly thought, "Perhaps Harry ISN'T the best at everything. Perhaps you don't have to be big to be the best."

Dodo felt very excited. "Perhaps I could be the best at something," she told herself.

But what?

Dodo thought really hard. "I know," she said at last. "I'm good at running. And I'm much lighter than Harry, so perhaps I could run faster." She thought of Harry's great big legs and enormous feet and felt a little unsure of herself.

Then she cheered up. "I'll never know if I don't try," she decided. "From now on, I'll run every day until I am really fit. Then I'll challenge Harry to a race."

Every morning after that, Dodo went out running.

She ran up and down the road . . .

over the hills and far away down to the big tree by the river . . .

Then she ran back again.

She ran
when it
was hot
and sunny
and she
was
puffing . . .

She ran
when it
was wet
and cold
and she
was
shivering.

She ran when she didn't really
feel like it . . .

and even
when she
got a stitch
in her side.

But every day she practiced,
and every day she got better
and better and faster and faster.

All this time, Harry just sat around, bossing the other dinosaurs and watching TV.

CHAPTER 3
The Race

When Dodo felt she was ready,
she took a deep breath and
walked right up to Harry.
"Harry," she said, "I'll bet I'm
better at running than you are."

Harry laughed scornfully.
"Don't be silly," he said.
"I'm the best at everything."

"No, you're not," said Dodo. "I'm the best at running now."

"I'll bet you're not," yelled Harry, getting angry.

Dodo moved well out of the way of Harry's tail.

"Then let's have a race," she said.

"All right," roared Harry. "When?"

"Now," said Dodo. "Right now.
I'll race you to the big tree by the
river and back again."

"Okay," said Harry, clambering to
his feet. "You're on."

He lumbered over to where Dodo
was standing.

"Who will say, *ready, set, go?*"
asked Dodo.

"I will," said one of the smaller
dinosaurs.

"Thank you," said Dodo.

The other dinosaurs crowded
around and watched as Harry
bounced up and down and
showed off his muscles.

"Ready

Set

GO!"

shouted Dodo's friend.

Harry tried to hit Dodo with his tail, but she was too quick. Off she raced with Harry thumping along beside her.

"Go, Dodo, go!" everyone yelled.

Harry soon ran out of breath and had to keep stopping to pant and hold his side. Too much TV-watching had made him very unfit. The dinosaurs couldn't believe their eyes. They shouted and cheered excitedly as Dodo raced to the lead.

"Look at Dodo run!" they hollered.

Nobody cheered for Harry.

Dodo ran and ran and ran and soon she was well ahead of Harry.

"Keep it up, Dodo!" shouted all the dinosaurs as she raced back to the finish.

And then they gathered around her hugging her and patting her on the back.

"Wow! What a runner!" everyone said.

"Look at poor old Harry. He's just no good, is he?"

Well, after that Harry didn't shout, "I'm the best," or "Make way for Harry," anymore. And he said, "Please," and "Thank you," just like Dodo.

He still didn't look where he put his feet, but it didn't matter. There were no tails to walk on because all the other dinosaurs were out jogging with Dodo every day.

It was much more fun than being pushed around by Harry.

More Popcorn Fantasies
by Pat Edwards

Don't Touch It, Lily
Lily didn't take any notice
when Gram told her not to
touch the vacuum cleaner.
But oh, what trouble it caused!

Mr. Mancini's Rats
When the rats move in,
they make life miserable for
Mr. Mancini and Fluffy.
There has to be a way to
get rid of them.
But what is it?

Three Wishes
When Ben meets a genie, he has
no idea that magic wishes can
go really wrong.
He soon finds out they can!